Easter Wonders: A Journey Through the World's Most Fascinating Traditions

Contents of the book:

Introduction:

Easter is one of the world's most widely celebrated holidays, yet how it is observed varies wildly across cultures, religions, and regions. In many countries, Easter is a time for reflection and renewal, a celebration of life's triumph over death, and a welcome embrace of spring's arrival. But beyond these common themes, the ways in which people celebrate this holiday are as diverse as humanity itself—each tradition offering a unique glimpse into the soul of a culture, a community, and its people.
In Easter Wonders, we set out to explore these remarkable customs, from the streets of Seville and their solemn Holy Week processions to the playful witch costumes of children in Finland. We dive deep into the symbolism behind Greece's midnight feasts, Guatemala's vibrant sawdust carpets, and the towering bonfires of Cyprus. Each page takes you on a journey to a different corner of the world, uncovering the history, symbolism, and spirit of traditions passed down through generations.
This book is more than a guide to Easter customs; it's an invitation to understand the universal themes of rebirth, hope, and unity that bind us all. Through these celebrations, communities honor the past, find joy in the present, and express their hopes for the future. In some places, the holiday is about spiritual .

reflection, as seen in the quiet blessings of Armenian families with dyed red eggs. In others, it's a jubilant event filled with community gatherings, music, and feasting, like Brazil's open-air reenactments and Italy's fiery "exploding carts." And everywhere, it's a time to connect—across family, friends, and neighbors—with acts of generosity, shared meals, and symbolic gifts.

This journey will take you from festive parades and meditative rituals to fields of wildflowers and kitchens filled with sweet, aromatic breads. We'll see how Easter has evolved over time, blending ancient beliefs with modern customs, and we'll celebrate the creativity and resilience of people who have transformed this holiday into a tapestry of unique traditions that enrich their cultures.

Whether you're reading to discover how others celebrate or looking for inspiration to add to your own traditions, Easter Wonders opens a window into the extraordinary ways the world welcomes the season of renewal. Let's journey together, marveling at the beauty, the mystery, and the joy of Easter as it unfolds in the lives and hearts of people everywhere.

Unique Easter traditions from around the world

Italy (Scoppio del Carro - "Explosion of the Cart"): In Florence, a centuries-old cart filled with fireworks is ignited in front of the Cathedral on Easter Sunday. This explosive tradition dates back to the Crusades, symbolizing both a blessing for a good harvest and the spiritual renewal of Easter. The fireworks symbolize light, hope, and celebration of Christ's resurrection.

Spain (Semana Santa Processions): During Semana Santa (Holy Week), especially in Seville, elaborate processions feature statues of Christ and the Virgin Mary. Participants wear long robes and hoods, carrying floats adorned with candles and flowers. This solemn ritual, often lasting late into the night, is a public display of penance, devotion, and reflection on Christ's sacrifice.

Germany (Osterbrunnen - Easter Wells): In some German villages, public fountains and wells are decorated with colorful eggs, flowers, and ribbons. This custom celebrates the importance of water as a life-giving resource and symbolizes renewal and purity. Communities come together to create beautiful displays, reinforcing bonds and celebrating the arrival of spring.

Greece (Easter Fireworks and "Pot Throwing"): In Corfu, Greeks celebrate Easter with a unique custom of throwing pots from their balconies. This tradition is thought to originate from Venetian rule and symbolizes the casting away of the old to make way for new growth and abundance. The clay pots crashing down also signify Christ breaking free from the tomb.

Finland (Easter Witches): Finnish children dress as witches and go door-to-door on Palm Sunday or Holy Saturday, asking for treats in exchange for willow branches they decorated with feathers and ribbons. This tradition combines religious and pagan elements, as the willow branches symbolize protection and the witches ward off evil.

France (Giant Omelet in Bessières): In the town of Bessières, residents prepare a giant omelet on Easter Monday using over 15,000 eggs. This tradition began when Napoleon and his troops stopped in the town, and he ordered an omelet for his soldiers. Now, it symbolizes abundance, community unity, and the sharing of food as a communal blessing.

Poland (Śmigus-Dyngus - Water Splashing): On Easter Monday, known as "Wet Monday," people splash each other with water, particularly young men dousing women. Traditionally, it was a courting ritual, but now it's a playful tradition that signifies the cleansing and renewal associated with spring and the Easter season.

Mexico (Passion Play in Iztapalapa): In Iztapalapa, a borough of Mexico City, locals perform one of the most famous Passion Plays in the world. Participants, some barefoot, reenact the crucifixion of Christ with great emotion, symbolizing sacrifice and devotion. The play, which attracts thousands of spectators, is a powerful expression of faith.

Ukraine (Kulich and Paskha): Ukrainians prepare special Easter foods, including Kulich (a tall, cylindrical bread) and Paskha (a sweet cheese dessert). The foods are blessed at church before being eaten. The round shape of Kulich and the white color of Paskha represent purity, rebirth, and the joy of Easter.

Philippines (Senakulo): Filipino towns host dramatic reenactments of Christ's Passion called Senakulo. This can include self-flagellation and even voluntary crucifixions as a form of penance. Participants believe it brings spiritual renewal, symbolizing gratitude for Christ's sacrifice.

Australia (Sydney Royal Easter Show): The Sydney Royal Easter Show is a major event that includes parades, animal displays, and entertainment, celebrating the agricultural heritage of Australia. Though not directly tied to Christian rituals, it reflects a national celebration of life and community during the Easter season.

Hungary (Sprinkling with Water): In Hungary, boys "sprinkle" girls with water or perfume on Easter Monday, traditionally symbolizing fertility and purity. The custom stems from ancient beliefs that water is a life-giving force, and this playful ritual has endured as a sign of new beginnings.

Romania (Red Eggs and Egg Battles): Romanians paint eggs, especially in red, symbolizing the blood of Christ. Families then participate in "egg battles," where two people hit their eggs together, and whoever's egg doesn't crack is considered blessed with good fortune.

United Kingdom (Egg Rolling): In the UK, children participate in egg rolling contests on Easter Sunday, where they roll eggs down a hill. The egg represents the stone rolled away from Christ's tomb, and the activity is a symbolic reenactment of the resurrection.

Sweden (Easter Witches and Bonfires): Swedish children dress up as Easter witches and visit neighbors for treats, similar to Halloween. In some areas, bonfires are lit to ward off evil spirits, symbolizing the end of darkness and the beginning of new life with spring.

Bermuda (Easter Kite Festival): Bermudians celebrate Good Friday by flying kites, often made in elaborate designs with bright colors. The kite is seen as a symbol of Christ's ascension, representing hope and the spirit's ability to rise.

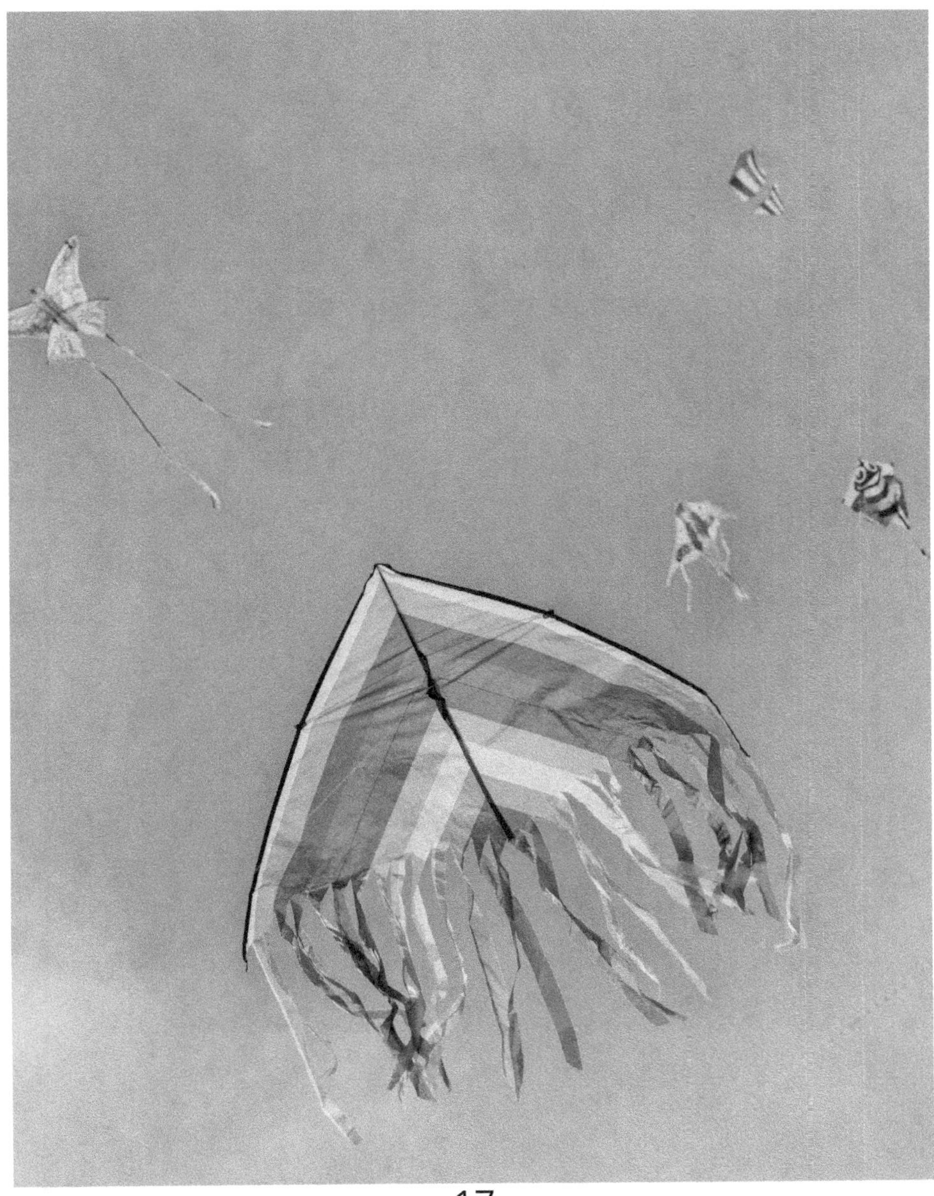

Israel (Via Dolorosa Procession): In Jerusalem, pilgrims walk the Via Dolorosa, the path Jesus took to Golgotha. This deeply spiritual journey symbolizes the trials and ultimate triumph of Christ's sacrifice, drawing believers from around the world.

Armenia (Blessing of Eggs): In Armenia, people bring decorated eggs to church for a blessing. Eggs symbolize the resurrection, with red eggs specifically representing the blood of Christ. Armenians then share these eggs with family and friends as blessings for health and fortune.

Switzerland (Egg Tossing Games): In some Swiss villages, people gather for an egg-tossing competition. The goal is to toss an egg as far as possible without breaking it, symbolizing resilience and strength. The winner is often believed to receive a year of good luck.

Colombia (Monserrate Pilgrimage): Colombians make a pilgrimage to the Monserrate Hill in Bogotá, where a church stands on the summit. This challenging trek symbolizes penance, faith, and dedication to Christ. Many pilgrims make the journey barefoot as a sign of humility and reverence.

Japan (Hanami and Easter Together): Although Easter is not widely celebrated in Japan, some Christian communities combine the season with "Hanami" (cherry blossom viewing), symbolizing the fragility of life and the beauty of rebirth, connecting nature with the resurrection.

United States (Easter Parade on Fifth Avenue, NYC):
New Yorkers celebrate Easter with a colorful parade along Fifth Avenue, featuring extravagant hats and costumes. Originally a religious procession, it has evolved into a vibrant, festive celebration of spring, symbolizing rebirth and self-expression.

Egypt (Sham El-Nessim): Egyptians celebrate Sham El-Nessim, an ancient spring festival with roots in Pharaonic times. People picnic and eat salted fish, green onions, and eggs, symbolizing life and fertility. It's celebrated the day after Easter, reflecting renewal and the start of a new season.

Brazil (Procissão do Encontro): During Holy Week, Brazilian communities reenact the meeting of Jesus and Mary on the way to the cross in a procession called Procissão do Encontro. This ritual signifies the sorrow and sacrifice of Christ's journey and Mary's mourning, showing a deep connection to family and faith.

Norway (Påskekrim - Easter Crime Fiction): In Norway, people have a unique Easter tradition of reading or watching crime stories, known as påskekrim (Easter crime). Bookstores even release special crime novels for Easter. This custom, which started with a crime novel advertisement in the 1920s, symbolizes mystery, contemplation, and entertainment during the Easter break.

Czech Republic (Pomlázka): On Easter Monday, Czech boys "gently" whip girls with braided willow rods called Pomlázka. The custom is believed to bring health and youth to women, drawing on ancient fertility rites to celebrate the arrival of spring.

Bulgaria (Egg Cracking Contest):
Bulgarians paint eggs in vibrant colors, and families participate in a contest where each person cracks their egg against another's. The one with the unbroken egg is believed to have a year of good fortune. This tradition symbolizes resilience and good luck, echoing themes of survival and renewal.

Ethiopia (Fasika):
For Ethiopian Orthodox Christians, Easter, or Fasika, is celebrated with a unique ritual that begins with a long Lent fast, avoiding all animal products. After midnight mass, families feast on doro wat (spicy chicken stew) and injera (sourdough flatbread). This feast marks the end of Lent and the joy of resurrection.

Slovakia (Whipping and Watering):

Slovak boys visit homes and "whip" girls with braided willow branches, often followed by splashing them with water. This tradition, similar to Hungary's, is thought to bring health, beauty, and vitality to women. It combines pagan and Christian beliefs, symbolizing the rejuvenating power of spring.

Netherlands (Paasvuren - Easter Fires):

In the eastern Netherlands, large bonfires called Paasvuren are lit on Easter Sunday. This custom dates back to pagan rituals for warding off evil spirits, with the flames symbolizing light's triumph over darkness. Villagers gather to watch, socialize, and celebrate the coming of spring.

Portugal (Compasso):

In Portugal, Compasso, a small procession, visits each home, where priests bless the residents and their families. This house blessing is meant to bring peace and prosperity, symbolizing Christ entering homes and hearts after resurrection.

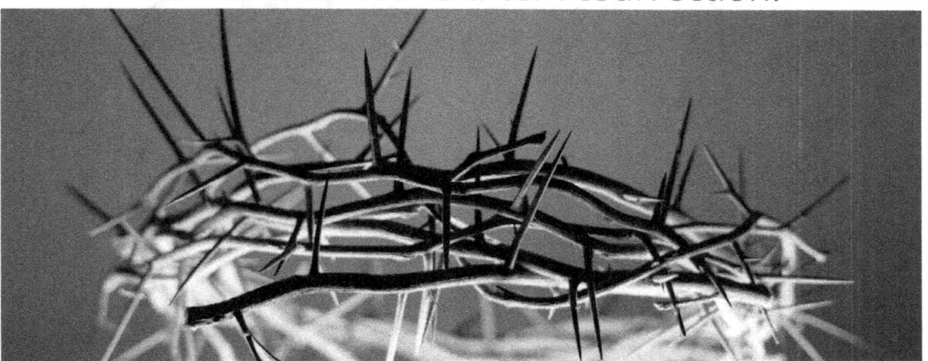

In Maltese towns, Easter Sunday is marked by a unique procession where men run through the streets carrying statues of the Risen Christ. This vigorous display, accompanied by joyous shouts, symbolizes the triumph of resurrection and the joy of new life.

India (Goan Easter Celebrations):

In Goa, Easter is celebrated with street processions, feasts, and fireworks. Goan Catholics prepare sorpotel (a spicy pork dish) and bebinca (a layered dessert) as part of the celebrations. The community aspect and shared meals represent unity, joy, and new beginnings.

Denmark (Gækkebreve - Guessing Letters):

Danish children send anonymous poems or gækkebreve, decorated letters with riddles, to friends or family. If the recipient guesses the sender, the sender owes them an egg. This playful tradition emphasizes connection, mystery, and the joy of giving.

Venezuela (Burning of Judas):

In Venezuela, people burn effigies of Judas on Easter Saturday. This represents the betrayal of Christ but has become a way to symbolically eliminate negativity, symbolizing renewal and justice, leaving room for peace and hope with the resurrection.

Czech Republic (Kraslice - Decorated Eggs):
Czechs create beautiful, intricate egg designs called kraslice using a wax-resist method. These eggs are exchanged as blessings for health, love, and new beginnings. This tradition highlights artistic expression and celebrates life's renewal.

Ireland (Herring Burial):
In Ireland, some coastal towns "bury" a herring on Good Friday, symbolizing the end of the Lenten fish diet. This humorous act reflects the transition from fasting to feasting, with fish symbolizing hardship and meat symbolizing celebration.

Slovenia (Easter Bread - Potica):

Slovenians bake Potica, a nut-filled Easter bread that's often blessed in church before being eaten. The spiral shape of Potica represents eternity, and sharing it with family symbolizes unity and love during the Easter feast.

Cyprus (Bonfire Competition):

In Cyprus, villages hold a bonfire competition on Easter Sunday. Bonfires, made from wooden crosses, are lit in the evening. This tradition, with roots in ancient Greek celebrations, symbolizes the victory of light over darkness and the resurrection.

El Salvador (Saw-Dust Carpets):

In the streets of El Salvador, intricate, colorful sawdust carpets are made during Holy Week. The carpets depict religious scenes and are crafted with dedication and artistry. They symbolize sacrifice, with the ephemeral art being destroyed as processions pass over it.

Peru (Pachamanca Feast):

In Peru's Andean regions, Easter Sunday is celebrated with a Pachamanca feast, where meat and vegetables are slow-cooked underground with hot stones. The meal celebrates life, honoring the earth and Christ's sacrifice.

Lebanon (Egg Cracking and Salib):

Lebanese Christians play a game of "egg tapping," breaking eggs symbolizing victory over death. Some families also tie palm crosses, known as salib, symbolizing faith and protection. The egg breaking symbolizes resilience and the power of faith.

Sicily, Italy (Diavolata):

In the town of Adrano, Sicily, locals perform the Diavolata, a play representing the battle between good (Christ) and evil (Satan). This theatrical performance symbolizes the victory of resurrection over death and is celebrated with music and festivities.

Serbia (Easter Fire):

In some Serbian regions, people light Easter fires on Holy Saturday. The flame represents the light of Christ, and villagers dance and sing around it, marking the resurrection with community bonding and celebration.

Jordan (Palm Procession):
In Jordan, particularly in Madaba, locals celebrate Palm Sunday with a palm procession. Participants wave palms, symbolizing Jesus' arrival in Jerusalem and the start of Holy Week. This procession represents welcoming, unity, and reverence.

Puerto Rico (El Jueves Santo - The Washing of the Feet):
On Holy Thursday, Puerto Rican churches hold reenactments of the washing of the feet, a ritual symbolizing humility and service to others. It reflects Christ's teachings on love and service to one another.

Greenland (Traditional Inuit Easter):

In Greenland, Easter is celebrated with special church services and social gatherings. Traditional Inuit hymns are sung, symbolizing the harmony of spiritual beliefs with nature and community, reflecting the renewal of life with the season.

Georgia (Decorating Red Eggs):

Georgians decorate eggs in red, representing Christ's blood. These are taken to church to be blessed, and then cracked to symbolize resurrection. The tradition reflects the themes of sacrifice, protection, and the strength of faith.

Nepal (Christian Processions):

In Nepal, the small Christian community holds Easter processions and services, often including Nepali hymns and traditional music. This celebration of the resurrection blends local culture with Christian spirituality, symbolizing hope amidst diversity.

Lithuania (Easter Palm Blessing):

Lithuanians bring intricately woven palms to church on Palm Sunday, symbolizing Christ's entry into Jerusalem. The palms are kept at home, believed to bring blessings and protection for the year.

Uganda (Traditional Dance and Music):
In Uganda, Easter is celebrated with music, dance, and feasts. Traditional dances reflect joy and praise, celebrating the resurrection and the victory of life over death. Feasts include locally sourced foods, symbolizing gratitude and community.

Switzerland (Eiertütschen - Egg Tapping):
In Switzerland, families engage in Eiertütschen, an egg-tapping contest where participants try to crack each other's eggs. The last intact egg symbolizes good fortune and resilience, celebrating survival and strength.

Macedonia (Burning Judas Effigy):

In Macedonia, communities burn effigies of Judas on Holy Saturday, symbolizing the cleansing of betrayal and sin. The flames represent forgiveness, renewal, and a fresh start with Christ's resurrection.

Zambia (Early Morning Prayers):

In Zambia, Easter begins with a sunrise prayer service. The early morning symbolizes new beginnings, and the congregation's joy represents the light and hope brought by Christ's resurrection.

Argentina (Carrying Palm Crosses):

Argentinians weave palms into crosses for Palm Sunday. These crosses are blessed and taken home as a symbol of faith, often kept to bring blessings throughout the year.

Estonia (Egg Dyeing with Onion Skins):

In Estonia, people dye eggs using natural materials like onion skins, which give the eggs a rich, reddish-brown color. The process of boiling and transforming the eggs represents new life and the resurrection, blending simplicity with symbolism.

Culinary Easter Traditions

Easter meals are rich in symbolism, often marking the end of Lent with celebratory feasts, and including dishes that represent renewal, fertility, and faith.

Italy (Colomba Pasquale):
Italians bake Colomba Pasquale, a dove-shaped sweet bread similar to panettone but flavored with almonds and sugar. The dove represents peace and the Holy Spirit, while the bread's sweetness and light texture reflect the joy of resurrection.

Greece (Magiritsa Soup):

After the midnight Easter service, Greeks traditionally break their Lenten fast with Magiritsa, a lamb and lemon soup. This soup is symbolic of Christ as the sacrificial lamb, representing new life and the transition from fasting to feasting.

Spain (Torrijas):

In Spain, torrijas—a dish similar to French toast—is enjoyed during Holy Week. Slices of bread soaked in milk and egg, then fried and dusted with cinnamon or honey, symbolize the sweetness of Easter, contrasting with the somber fast of Lent.

Ukraine (Kulitch and Paskha): Ukrainians prepare Kulitch, a tall, cylindrical bread often decorated with icing, and Paskha, a sweet cheese mold traditionally made with raisins and candied fruits. These are blessed in church before being eaten, symbolizing purity, resurrection, and the joy of Easter.

United Kingdom (Hot Cross Buns):
In the UK, hot cross buns are traditionally eaten on Good Friday. The cross on top represents the crucifixion, and spices inside recall the burial spices used on Christ. Sharing these buns with family or neighbors symbolizes goodwill and unity.

Portugal (Folar):

Folar is a Portuguese bread baked with whole eggs (shell and all) nestled on top, representing rebirth and fertility. It's a symbolic gift that people share with family or close friends, reinforcing bonds and celebrating new life.

During Holy Week, Mexicans prepare Capirotada, a bread pudding made with cinnamon, cloves, and cheese, symbolizing the passion of Christ. The bread represents Christ's body, the syrup His blood, and spices the burial spices, turning the dish into a profound reminder of sacrifice.

Poland (Babka and Mazurek):

Polish Easter tables often feature Babka, a tall, yeasted cake, and Mazurek, a flat pastry decorated with nuts and dried fruits. The circular Babka represents eternal life, while the festive decorations on Mazurek symbolize the joy of resurrection.

Argentinians enjoy Rosca de Pascua, a ring-shaped sweet bread topped with pastry cream and sometimes candied fruit. Its round shape symbolizes eternal life and unity, and it's often enjoyed with family as a celebration of resurrection.

Ethiopia (Doro Wat):

Ethiopian Orthodox Christians break their Lent fast with Doro Wat, a spicy chicken stew served with injera. This dish represents abundance and life, celebrating the end of fasting with a flavorful, communal meal.

Finland (Mämmi):
Mämmi, a rye-based pudding served with cream or milk, is a Finnish Easter delicacy. Its dark, earthy flavor reflects the season's solemnity, and it's served during Easter as a reminder of humility and simplicity.

In France, people enjoy Oeufs en Cocotte, baked eggs in cream and herbs, for Easter. Eggs are central to Easter in France, symbolizing fertility, life, and rebirth.

Unique Easter Clothing

Many countries have distinctive clothing traditions for Easter, often representing purity, renewal, or local cultural elements.

Spain (Nazarenos in Semana Santa):
In Spanish Semana Santa processions, participants wear Nazareno outfits, which include hooded robes of various colors depending on the brotherhood. These robes represent penance and anonymity, allowing participants to reflect humbly on Christ's Passion.

United States (Easter Bonnets and Parade Hats):
The Easter Bonnet tradition, especially in the U.S. (like the Fifth Avenue parade in New York City), involves elaborate, often whimsical hats. These hats symbolize joy and the freshness of spring, with many hats decorated in flowers and ribbons.

Italy (Traditional White Clothes for Baptisms):
Italians often wear white for Easter baptisms, as Easter is a popular time for these ceremonies. White represents purity and new life, reflecting the Christian theme of rebirth and renewal.

Philippines (All White for Salubong):
Filipinos often wear white for the Salubong ceremony, a reenactment of the risen Christ meeting the Virgin Mary. The color represents purity, resurrection, and new beginnings.

Ethiopia (Netela Cloth):
Ethiopian Orthodox Christians wear traditional white Netela cloths to church on Easter Sunday. This garment, draped over the shoulders, symbolizes reverence, purity, and humility during the holy celebration.

Bulgaria (Bright Traditional Costumes):

In Bulgaria, people wear traditional embroidered costumes featuring bright colors on Easter Sunday. These costumes represent joy and celebration, with red threads symbolizing life and resurrection.

Greece (New Clothes for Easter Sunday):
Greeks often wear new clothes on Easter Sunday, symbolizing a fresh start and new life. Children especially receive new clothes as a blessing, reflecting the new beginning that Easter represents.

Romania (Folk Costumes for Easter Sunday):
In rural Romanian communities, people wear traditional folk costumes with intricate embroidery to Easter Mass. The costumes' bright colors and patterns represent life, renewal, and the joy of the resurrection.

Hungary (Embroidered Blouses and Skirts):

Hungarian women wear beautifully embroidered blouses and skirts on Easter Sunday, often in celebration of spring and new life. These clothes symbolize beauty, fertility, and cultural heritage, blending faith with folklore.

Gift-Giving Traditions and Symbolism

Easter gifts often carry religious, cultural, or symbolic meanings, representing blessings, joy, and goodwill.

Ukraine (Pysanky Eggs):

Ukrainians give intricately decorated Pysanky eggs to family and friends. Each design holds specific meanings, such as protection, health, and fertility. This gift-giving symbolizes blessings and sharing goodwill.

Poland (*Święconka Baskets*):

Polish families prepare Święconka baskets filled with symbolic foods like eggs, bread, and salt, which are blessed on Holy Saturday and then shared. Each food represents a blessing, from health to abundance, and the baskets are gifts of prosperity.

France (Chocolate Fish and Bells):

French children receive chocolate fish and bells as Easter gifts, symbols of Christ and the "flying bells" that return on Easter morning after "leaving" on Holy Thursday. These gifts represent faith and joy.

Germany (Osterhase Gifts):

The Osterhase (Easter hare) leaves eggs and treats for German children, marking the start of spring. Eggs and rabbits symbolize fertility and new beginnings, and these gifts encourage hope and joy.

United States (Easter Baskets):

American children receive Easter baskets filled with candies, toys, and chocolate eggs. The eggs and spring themes represent rebirth, while the treats celebrate joy and the end of Lent.

Sweden (Decorated Eggs and Sweets):
Swedes give one another colorful eggs filled with candy. These eggs, often intricately decorated, symbolize spring, renewal, and the return of light after a long winter.

Mexico (Capirotada for Family and Friends):
Mexicans share Capirotada, a sweet bread pudding, as a gift to loved ones. Each ingredient has symbolic meaning related to the Passion of Christ, and sharing this dessert represents love, sacrifice, and community.

Greece (Easter Candles - Lambades):
Greek children receive Lambades, elaborately decorated candles gifted by their godparents for Easter. These candles, used during the Resurrection service, symbolize the light of Christ and the bond between godparent and child.

Slovakia (Decorated Eggs as Friendship Tokens):

Slovaks exchange decorated eggs, symbolizing friendship and goodwill. These eggs are given to family, friends, and even as romantic gestures, representing blessings, love, and new beginnings.

Brazil (Chocolate Easter Eggs):

Brazilians give large, hollow chocolate eggs to friends and family, filled with smaller treats or messages. The egg symbolizes new life, and the gift represents joy and the love shared with family.

Italy (Colomba Cake for Friends and Neighbors):

Italians gift Colomba Pasquale, a dove-shaped cake, to family, friends, and neighbors. The dove represents peace, and the sharing of this cake symbolizes love, hope, and unity within the

Lebanon (Decorated Eggs for Family Members):
Lebanese Christians give decorated eggs as Easter
gifts, a token of hope, fertility, and health. Each egg
represents a unique blessing, shared within the
family to wish them a joyful year.

Final Thoughts and Farewell

As our journey through the world's most fascinating Easter traditions comes to an end, we hope this book has transported you to places you may not have known, introduced you to customs you may not have imagined, and deepened your appreciation for the ways in which people celebrate the beauty of life, faith, and renewal. Each tradition tells a story—of community, resilience, and a shared spirit that transcends geography and language, uniting people through symbols of hope and rebirth.

Perhaps along the way, you've discovered an Easter custom that resonates with you or that you'd like to try with your own family and friends. Traditions, after all, thrive when they're shared and cherished, adapted by each generation in new and meaningful ways. And as you reflect on the stories in these pages, we hope you're inspired to create, celebrate, and connect with others in your own unique way.

We would love to hear about your experiences with this book—your thoughts, your favorite parts, or any traditions you may have discovered or revived along the way. Did a particular tradition stand out to you? Did a specific cultural story move you? Your feedback not only helps us create books that resonate with readers but also keeps the spirit of Easter Wonders alive.

Please share your thoughts, insights, and experiences by leaving a review. Your feedback is a valuable part of our journey together, and it helps us bring new perspectives and traditions to life for readers around the world. Thank you for joining us on this journey, and may each Easter bring new joy, connection, and wonder into your life.
Until next time, may the spirit of renewal and hope be with you always.

* 9 7 9 8 3 4 4 9 0 8 9 7 7 *